POCKET

QUEER

WISDOM

POCKET

QUEER

WISDOM

Inspirational quotes and wise words from
queer heroes who changed the world

Hardie Grant

B O O K S

CONTENTS

INTRODUCTION

Listen up: the queer heroes of music, art, theatre and literature have something to say. From tough-ass political activists to pop culture icons, discover the wise words of non-binary pioneers and gender non-conformists, gay codebreakers, trans revolutionaries, and lesbians in space.

Some have been all but ignored by history, misunderstood or taken too soon, while others have burned brightly, loud-mouthed and wonderfully precocious. There are those born into privilege who risk it all by coming out, and others that have clawed their way out of the mire with talent and tenacity.

What makes a queer hero? You don't have to be gay, lesbian, bisexual, trans or unicorn (although it helps). What's needed is a queer-minded attitude, being an ally to civil equality, living life to the fullest, and leaving a queer legacy so others in the future can climb ever higher.

What sets them apart is a steadfastness, a bravery to live life against the rules, to ignore social convention and risk everything, from reputations to lives, to change the world. In the following pages are some of their most magical words to give you guidance, strength, and a little sassiness: queer power in your pocket.

GILBERT BAKER

1951–2017

Gay activist and creator of the iconic rainbow flag

'We needed something to express our joy, our beauty, our power. And the rainbow did that.'

FREDDIE MERCURY

1946–91

Frontman of legendary pop-rock outfit Queen

'Boredom and dullness
are diseases.'

CHRISTOPHER ISHERWOOD

1904–86

Author of *Goodbye to Berlin* and *A Single Man*

'Only those capable of silliness can be called truly intelligent.'

from *Christopher and His Kind*, 1976

RADCLYFFE HALL

1880–1943

Taboo-breaking, gender-busting poet and novelist

'Do try to remember this: even the world's not so black as it's painted.'

from *The Well of Loneliness*, 1928

KD LANG

Born 1961

Canadian country singer-songwriter

'Androgyny to me is making your sexuality available, through your art, to everyone.'

KEITH HARING

1958–90

American artist and social activist

'Art should be something that liberates your soul, provokes the imagination and encourages people to go further.'

BARBARA GITTINGS

1932–2007

Civil rights pioneer and the grande dame of
the modern LGBTQI+ rights movement

'Equality means more than passing laws. The struggle is really won in the hearts and minds of the community, where it really counts.'

RUPAUL

Born 1960

American drag queen and shrewd owner
of a media empire

'Whatever other people think of me is none of my business.'

CHAVELA VARGAS

1919–2012

Latin American icon and Mexican chanteuse

'**When you like something, you should do it all night long.**'

SALLY RIDE

1951–2012

Physicist, science educator and the first
American woman to fly in space

On men versus women
in astronaut training

'Weightlessness is a great equalizer.'

JAMES BALDWIN

1924–87

American writer, essayist and social commentator

'Not everything that is faced can be changed; but nothing can be changed until it is faced.'

QUENTIN CRISP

1908–99

Pastel-hued English actor, writer and raconteur

'Never keep up with the Joneses. Drag them down to your level.'

GERTRUDE STEIN

1874–1946

American novelist, poet, playwright, and art collector

'One does not get better but different and older and that is always a pleasure.'

HARVEY MILK

1930–78

American politician and the first openly gay
person elected to public office in California

'If a bullet should enter my brain, let that bullet destroy every closet door in the country.'

VIRGINIA WOOLF

1882–1941

Feminist, Bloomsbury group scenester and one of the
most important authors of 20th century Modernism

'No need to hurry.
No need to sparkle.
No need to be anybody
but oneself.'

from 'A Room of One's Own', 1929

LILI ELBE

1882–1931

Danish artist and gender pioneer

'I, Lili, am vital and have a right to life.'

ANDY WARHOL

1928–87

American artist, director, producer and
pioneer of the Pop Art movement

'If you can convince yourself that you look fabulous, you can save yourself the trouble of primping.'

BILLIE HOLIDAY

1915–59

Iconic American jazz and blues singer

'Without feeling, whatever you do amounts to nothing.'

DAN SAVAGE

Born 1964

Radical sex-advice columnist and
podcaster of *Savage Love* fame

'It gets better.'

AUDRE LORDE

1934–92

Poet, feminist, activist and 'crazy and queer' hero

'Your silence will not protect you.'

SANDRA BERNHARD

Born 1955

American performer, author and activist

'I'm not gonna change. I'm not gonna get a nose job. I'm not going to pretend I'm the girl next door ... But I do live in the neighbourhood, so you better get used to me.'

RON WOODROOF

1950–92

Ultimate drugstore cowboy, life-saver and
founder of the Dallas Buyers Club

'I am my own physician.'

CANDY DARLING

1944–1974

Glamorous trans woman, actress,
scenester and muse to Andy Warhol

'I'm a thousand different people. Every one is real.'

OSCAR WILDE

1854–1900

Irish poet, novelist and playwright

'We are all in the gutter, but some of us are looking at the stars.'

from *Lady Windermere's Fan*, 1893

LILY TOMLIN

Born 1939

American actor, comedian, singer and activist

'I always wondered why somebody doesn't do something about that. Then I realised I was somebody.'

ALAN TURING

1912–54

Genius computer scientist and saviour of the world

'We can only see a short distance ahead, but we can see plenty there that needs to be done.'

MICHAEL DILLON

1915–62

Gender warrior, doctor, writer, surgical pioneer,
hero of the Blitz, and Buddhist monk

'There is space in the universe for all types.'

MADONNA

Born 1958

Queen of pop, activist and ultimate gay icon

'I'm tough, ambitious, and I know exactly what I want. If that makes me a bitch, okay.'

RACHEL MADDOW

Born 1973

American television host, political commentator,
writer and Emmy-award winner

'Don't focus on what I'm wearing. Focus on what's coming out of my face.'

LARRY KRAMER

Born 1935

Award-winning writer, playwright and troublemaker

'Nothing works for everybody.'

from *The Normal Heart and the Destiny of Me*, 1992

LAVERNE COX

Born 1972

Actor, performer, writer, producer
and civil rights activist

'I think transpeople show everyone that you can define what it means to be a man or woman on your own terms.'

CAMILLE PAGLIA

Born 1947

Academic, critic, and all-round queer badass

'My advice, as in everything, is to read widely and think for yourself.'

STEPHEN TENNANT

1906–87

Socialite, muse and silk-dressing-gowned
30s party boy

On fat shamers –

'But I'm beautiful! And the more of me there is the better I like it!'

ALLEN GINSBERG

1926–97

American poet, philosopher, activist,
and pioneer of the Beat Generation

'Follow your inner moonlight; don't hide the madness.'

ELLEN DEGENERES

Born 1958

Comic, talk show host, actor and business-leader

'Do things that make you happy within the confines of the legal system.'

MARLENE DIETRICH

1901–92

Legendary Hollywood star,
German actor and singer

'At the best of times gender is difficult to determine.'

ARMISTEAD MAUPIN

Born 1944

American novelist

'Being gay has taught me tolerance, compassion and humility. It has shown me limitless possibilities of living.'

from *More Tales of the City*, 1980

ELEANOR ROOSEVELT

1884–1962

Political figure, diplomat, activist and the First Lady
of the United States of America 1933–45

'No one can make you feel inferior without your consent.'

JUSTIN VIVIAN BOND

Born 1963

Award-winning American singer-songwriter,
author, artist, actor and activist

'I think everybody's trans.'

SYLVIA RIVERA

1951–2002

American gay liberation and transgender activist,
drag queen and veteran of the 1969 Stonewall uprising

'Hell hath no fury like a drag queen scorned.'

GEORGE TAKEI

Born 1937

Galaxy-hopping Japanese American actor,
writer, director and *bon vivant*

'We should indeed keep calm in the face of difference, and live our lives in a state of inclusion and wonder at the diversity of humanity.'

FRIDA KAHLO

1907–54

Mexican painter, feminist and thinker

'At the end of the day,
we can endure much
more than we think
we can.'

PETER TATCHELL

Born 1952

Australian-born, British human rights campaigner

'Don't accept the world as it is. Dream about what the world could be – and then help make it happen.'

SOURCES

Aarons, D. 2012, *Jokes and the Linguistic Mind*, Routledge – **p. 57**

Balderston, D & D. J. Guy (Eds.) 1997, *Sex and Sexuality in Latin America*, New York University Press – p. **25**

Baldwin, J. 1962, 'As Much Truth as One Can Bear', *New York Times Book Review* – p. **29**

Barr, R. 2012, 'Sandra Bernhard', *Interview Magazine* (online), viewed 10 Jan 2018, www.interviewmagazine.com – p. **49**

Bennetts, L. 1993, 'k. d. lang Cuts It Close', *Vanity Fair* (online), viewed 10 Jan 2019, www.vanityfair.com – p. **17**

Brandreth, G. (Ed.) 2013, *Oxford Dictionary of Humorous Quotations*, Oxford University Press – p. **31**

Brooks, G. & S. Lupton (Eds.) 2008, *Freddie Mercury: His Life in His Own Words*, Omnibus Press – p. **11**

Bruccoli, M. J., S. Fitzgerald Smith & J. P. Kerr (Eds.) 1974, *The Romantic Egoists: A Pictorial Autobiography from the Scrapbooks and Albums of F. Scott and Zelda Fitzgerald*, University of South Carolina Press – p. **33**

Chavez, N. 2017, 'Rainbow flag creator Gilbert Baker dies at 65', CNN, viewed 10 January 2019, edition.cnn.com – p. **9**

Couric, K. 2011, 'Rachel Maddow Tells Katie Couric, "I'm Not Competing on the Pretty-Girl-on-Cable Front"', *Glamour* (online), viewed 10 Jan 2019, www.glamour.com – p. **65**

Cross, M. 2007, *Madonna, A Biography*, Greenwood Press – p. **63**

Darling, C. 1997, *My Face for the World to See: The Diaries, Letters, and Drawings of Candy Darling, Andy Warhol Superstar*, Hardy Marks Publications – p. **53**

DeGeneres, E. 2011, *Seriously . . . I'm Kidding*, Hachette – p. **77**

Dietrich, M. 2012, *Marlene Dietrich's ABC*, Open Road Media – p. **79**

Dillon, M. 1946, *Self: A Study in Ethics and Endocrinology*, William Heinemann Medical Books – p. **61**

Doonan, S. 2008, *Eccentric Glamour: Creating an Insanely More Fabulous You*, Simon & Schuster – p. **41**

Elbe, L. 2004, *Man into Woman*, Blue Boat Books – p. **39**

Glisson, S. M. (Ed.) 2006, *The Human Tradition in the Civil Rights Movement*, Rowman & Littlefield Publishers, Inc. – p. **87**

Hall, R. 2013, *The Well of Loneliness*, Read Books Ltd. – p. **15**

Haring, K. 2010, *Keith Haring Journals*, Penguin – p. **19**

Hoby, H. 2011, 'Justin Bond: 'I think everybody's trans'', *The Guardian*, viewed 10 Jan 2019, www.theguardian.com – p. **85**

Holiday, B. 1956, *Lady Sings the Blues*, Broadway Books – p. **43**

Isherwood, C. 2012, *Christopher and His Kind*, Vintage – p. **13**

Jacobson, S. 2013. 'The Real Dallas Buyers Club', *The Dallas Morning News*, viewed 8 Jan 2018, www.pressreader.com – p. **51**

Kramer, L. 2000, *The Normal Heart and the Destiny of Me*, Avalon Travel Publishing – p. **67**

Lorde, A. 1984, 'The Transformation of Silence into Language and Action', *Sister Outsider*, Ten Speed Press – p. **47**

Maupin, A. 1989, *More Tales from the City*, Black Swan – p. **81**

Paglia, C. 2018, *Free Women, Free Men: Sex, Gender, Feminism*, Canongate Books – p. **71**

Pocket Frida Kahlo Wisdom, Hardie Grant Books, 2018 – p. **91**

Romano, T. 2017, 'An Interview with Laverne Cox: "I Absolutely Consider Myself a Feminist"', *Here We Are: Feminism for the Real World*, ed. K. Jensen, Algonquin Books – p. **69**

Roosevelt, E. 2014, *This is My Story*, HarperCollins – p. **83**

RuPaul [@RuPaul], 2011, (2 Mar, 4.11 pm) 'What other people think of me is none of my business [Tweet], viewed 10 Jan 2018, www.twitter.com – p. **23**

Savage, D. & T. Miller (Eds.) 2016, *It Gets Better*, Penguin Books – p. **45**

Shilts, R. 2009, *The Mayor of Castro Street: The Life and Times of Harvey Milk*, Atlantic Books – p. **35**

Stevenson, R. 2016, *Pride: Celebrating Diversity & Community*, Orca Book Publishers – p. **21**

Strickland, B [Ed.] 1989, *On Being a Writer*, Writer's Digest Books – p. **75**

Swaby, R. 2016, *Trailblazers: 33 Women in Science Who Changed the World*, Delacorte Press – p. **27**

Takei, G. 2013, *Lions and Tigers and Bears (The Internet Strikes Back)*, Oh Myyy! Limited Liability Company – p. **89**

Tatchell, P. [@UsefulandKind], 2016, (25 Nov, 3.05 am) "Don't accept the world as it is. Dream of what the world could be - and then help make it happen" [Tweet], viewed 10 Jan 2018, www.twitter.com – p. **93**

Turing, A. 2004, 'Computing Machinery and Intelligence', *The Essential Turing*, ed. B. J. Copeland, Oxford University Press – p. **59**

Waters, J. 1991, 'The Man Who Stayed in Bed', *The New York Times Book Review*, Vol. 96 – p. **73**

Wilde, O. 2008, *Lady Windemere's Fan, The Importance of Being Earnest and Other Plays*, Oxford University Press, ed. P. Raby – p. **55**

Woolf, W. 2015, 'A Room of One's Own', *A Room of One's Own and Three Guineas*, Oxford University Press – p. **37**

Pocket Queer Wisdom

Published in 2019 by Hardie Grant Books,
an imprint of Hardie Grant Publishing

Hardie Grant Books (London)
5th & 6th Floors
52–54 Southwark Street
London SE1 1UN

Hardie Grant Books (Melbourne)
Building 1, 658 Church Street
Richmond, Victoria 3121

hardiegrantbooks.com

British Library Cataloguing-in-Publication Data. A catalogue
record for this book is available from the British Library.

ISBN: 978-1-78488-285-3

Publisher: Kate Pollard
Junior Editor: Rebecca Fitzsimons
Designer: Studio Noel
Illustrator: Michele Rosenthal

Colour Reproduction by p2d
Printed and bound in China by Leo Paper Group